Dinosaur
Alphabet

by David West

Crabtree Publishing Company
www.crabtreebooks.com

Author: David West
Editor: Crystal Sikkens
Editorial director: Kathy Middleton
Prepress technician: Margaret Salter
Cover design: Margaret Salter
Image credits: David West
Cover credits: Shutterstock (background); David West

Published in 2013 by CRABTREE PUBLISHING COMPANY

Library and Archives Canada Cataloguing in Publication

West, David, 1956-
    Dinosaur alphabet / David West.

(I learn with dinosaurs)
Issued also in electronic formats.
ISBN 978-0-7787-7453-2 (bound).--ISBN 978-0-7787-7458-7 (pbk.)

    1. English language--Alphabet--Juvenile literature.
2. Dinosaurs--Juvenile literature. 3. Alphabet books. I. Title.
II. Series.: West, David, 1956- I learn with dinosaurs.

PE1155.W48 2013   j421'.1   C2012-908486-7

Library of Congress Cataloging-in-Publication Data

CIP available at Library of Congress

Crabtree Publishing Company
www.crabtreebooks.com   1-800-387-7650

Printed in Canada/012013/MA20121217

Published in Canada
Crabtree Publishing
616 Welland Ave.
St. Catharines, Ontario
L2M 5V6

Published in the United States
Crabtree Publishing
PMB 59051
350 Fifth Avenue, 59th Floor
New York, New York 10118

Published in the United Kingdom
Crabtree Publishing
Maritime House
Basin Road North, Hove
BN41 1WR

Published in Australia
Crabtree Publishing
3 Charles Street
Coburg North
VIC, 3058

Aa

Alioramus

ah-lee-o-RAH-mus

Bb

Beipiaosaurus

bay-pyow-SAWR-us

Cc

Carnotaurus
kahrn-uh-TAWR-us

Dicraeosaurus

dye-CRAY-uh-SAWR-us

Ee

Edmontosaurus

ed-MON-tuh-SAWR-us

Fruitadens
FRUIT-ah-denz

Gg Giganotosaurus
gig-an-OH-toe-SAWR-us

Hh Huayangosaurus
hwah-YAHNG-o-SAWR-us

Ii Iguanodon
ig-WAN-oh-don

Jj Juravenator

JOO-ruh-ven-AY-tor

Kk Kentrosaurus
KEN-truh-SAWR-us

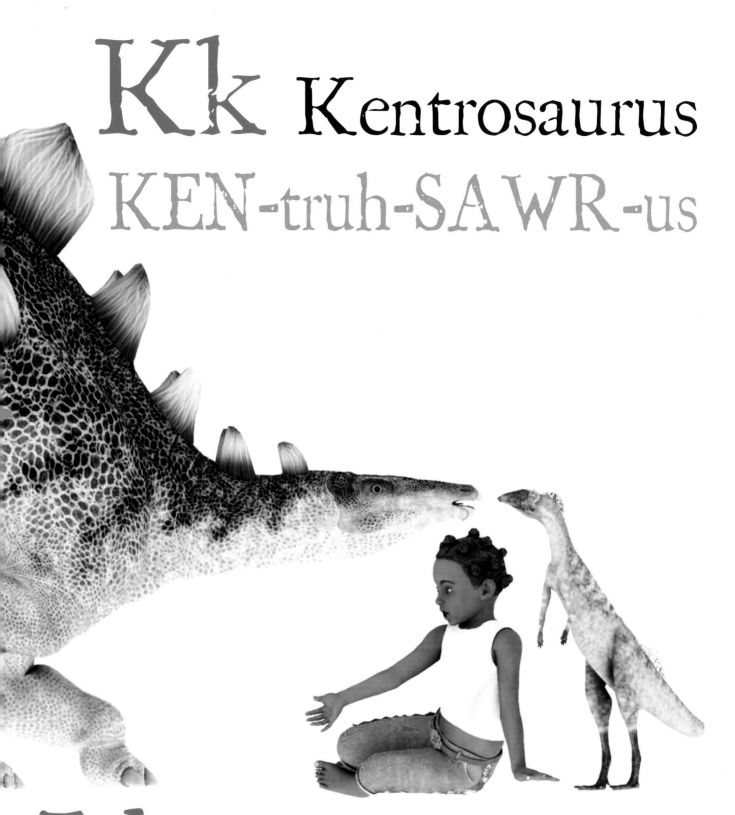

Ll Lesothosaurus
leh-SOTH-uh-SAWR-us

Mm

Megalosaurus
MEG-uh-lo-SAWR-us

Nanotyrannus

NAN-uh-tye-RAN-us

Oo

Olorotitan
oh-LOW-ruh-tye-tan

Parasaurolophus

par-ah-SAWR-OL-uh-fus

Qq

Qiupalong
KYOO-puh-long

Rugops
ROO-gops

Ss

Spinosaurus

SPY-nuh-SAWR-us

Tyrannosaurus

tye-RAN-uh-SAWR-us

Uu

Utahraptor
Yoo-tah-RAP-tor

V v

Velociraptor
veh-loss-ih-RAP-tor

Ww
Wuerhosaurus
WER-uh-
SAWR-us

Xx
Xuanhuaceratops
ZWAN-ha-SAIR-uh-tops

Yy

Yangchuanosaurus

yang-chew-ANN-uh-SAWR-us

Zz

Zuniceratops

zoo-nee-SAIR-uh-tops